D1537874

J
B
SELES

Goodman, Michael E.
Monica Seles

	DATE DUE		

2/98

Published by Creative Education
123 South Broad Street, Mankato, Minnesota 56001
Creative Education is an imprint of The Creative Company

Designed by Stephanie Blumenthal.

Photos by: Allsport Photography, Archive Photos, Associated Press/Wide World Photos,
Fotosport, Globe Photos, Anthony Neste, Silver Image, and SportsChrome.

Library of Congress Cataloging-in-Publication Data

Goodman, Michael E.
Monica Seles / by Michael E. Goodman.
p. cm. — (Ovations)
ISBN 0-88682-699-3

1. Seles, Monica, 1973- —Juvenile literature. 2. Tennis players—Yugoslavia—Biography—Juvenile
literature. 3. Women tennis players—Yugoslavia—Biography—Juvenile literature.
[1. Seles, Monica, 1973- . 2. Tennis players. 3. Women—Biography.] I. Title. II. Series.

GV994.S45G67 1997   93-49768
796.342'092
[B]—DC20

First edition

5 4 3 2 1

MONICA SELES

BY MICHAEL E. GOODMAN

Creative ☾ Education

REFLECTIONS

On the tennis court, she is all business and power. Her trademarks are a slashing two-handed forehand and a loud, impolite grunt that distracts opponents as much as it adds to her concentration. She never slows down, racing from one side of the court to the other, beating the ball to its destination and staying ahead of her opponent. Her tennis matches sometimes seem to resemble battles more than games.

The battles have become tougher since May 1993, when she was stabbed on the sidelines by a rabid fan. Her comeback to the game has been successful, but her innocence and pure joy in playing tennis may never return completely.

"Tennis is a game, a sport," she says. "All I ever wanted to do was to stay simple and play it."

She is a new breed of international athlete—born in Yugoslavia, trained in the United States, and recognized as a champion from Australia to France to the United States. Her rise to the top was phenomenal. By the age of eight, she was a national champion in Yugoslavia, and before age 18, she was ranked number one in the world. She moved ahead so quickly that tennis fans hardly knew her name before she was near the top of her sport. And even after staying away from tennis for more than two years following her stabbing, she returned as a champion.

Off the court, she can be playful or glamorous, mischievous or mysterious. The little girl in her is reflected in her collections of magazines, dolls, and stuffed animals. The elegant grown woman emerges when she dresses up in fine clothes and jewels. She dreams of someday being a "mystery woman" or a Hollywood star, aloof and secluded from the public. At the same time, she is always friendly to fans and reporters. She seems unspoiled by being in the spotlight, and still very proud of what she has accomplished.

With good humor and mental toughness she has conquered adversity, both on and off the court. She is a free spirit who is determined to be herself and not to fit someone else's pattern. Her future career options are nearly limitless, and so is her capacity for hard work.

This is Monica Seles, a young woman with a powerful, two-handed grip on success.

Monica Seles is an international star. She was born in Yugoslavia, trained in the United States, and has won tennis tournaments around the world.

E V O L U T I O N

Almost from the day Monica Seles was born—on December 2, 1973—her parents decided she would be an athlete. Monica's father, Karolj Seles, an award-winning political cartoonist and filmmaker in Yugoslavia, had been one of the top track stars in Europe as a young man. Her mother, Esther, was a computer programmer who also loved sports. The couple encouraged their two children, Zoltan and Monica, to get involved in athletics, especially tennis, at a young age.

Karolj Seles gave Monica her first racquet when she was six years old and began training her himself. Their first court was set up in a parking lot near the family's apartment in Novi Sad, Yugoslavia (now Serbia), with a string tied to the bumpers of two cars serving as

a net. Monica quickly became frustrated and said she wanted to quit tennis and return to playing with her dolls. When her 15-year-old brother Zoltan began winning tournaments and bringing home trophies, though, Monica's jealousy and competitive spirit soon took over. She told her father, "Let's go play tennis again."

Karolj Seles decided to make a few changes in his daughter's training methods to make the sport more fun for her to learn. He created a series of cartoon films to teach Monica fundamentals. Then he drew pictures of the cartoon characters Tom and Jerry onto the tennis balls Monica used during practice. Karolj explained to his child that "a tennis player must go after her opponent like Tom the cat goes after Jerry the mouse."

Monica's father added two more innovations to her training. First, he taught her to use a two-handed grip for both her backhand and forehand shots to get more power behind her strokes. Then he found a way to encourage Monica to hit shots more accurately. He put stuffed animals inside boxes

Monica's parents, Esther and Karolj Seles, encouraged their daughter to get involved in athletics at a young age. Monica received her first tennis racquet when she was six years old.

he drew on the court. If Monica hit five balls into a box, she would earn a doll as a prize.

First Monica's doll supply grew and then so did her trophy collection. At age eight, she won the Yugoslav Championships for players 12 years old and younger. At the time, Monica knew how to do almost everything on the court except keep score. In fact, her father had to tell her when the title match ended and who had won.

Before her ninth birthday arrived, Monica was regularly defeating many of Europe's top teenage players, including her older brother. Zoltan soon decided to give up tennis for other interests, but Monica kept working with her father and improving. Her trophies and honors began piling up. She won the 12-and-under division of the European Championships two years in a row. Then, in 1985, she became the youngest person ever to be named Yugoslavia's Sportswoman of the Year.

Monica has been collecting trophies and honors for years. In addition to her many tournament trophies, she has the honor of being the youngest person ever to be named Yugoslavia's Sportswoman of the Year.

During this time, Monica developed a new weapon to go along with her powerful strokes on the court—"The Grunt." As her racquet moved toward the ball, she would let out a loud "uuhhnn AAGGH!" sound from deep in her throat. The more important the point, the louder the grunt. It wasn't a very polite sound, but it did help her concentrate. "The Grunt" is still part of Monica's game today, though opponents and tennis officials have asked her to tone it down a little bit.

Despite Monica's increasing success, it was not easy for her to train in her home country. The nearest indoor courts were 90 minutes away, and there were few outdoor grass or hard courts around. In addition, Monica's father felt that she was getting too good for him to coach her properly by himself.

A solution to these problems presented itself when world famous tennis coach Nick Bollettieri invited Monica and her family to move to his tennis camp in Bradenton, Florida. The Seleses were now faced with an important decision. For Monica's parents and brother, a move to the United States would mean giving up their home and jobs and heading to a new country with a different language and customs. For Monica, it would mean having the opportunity to become one of the world's best tennis players. The family talked it over and decided to head to Florida.

"It's hard to have everything in your life," said Zoltan, discussing the move. "This was our choice. We came here because of Monica."

When she first arrived in Florida, Monica practiced against the other female players in the Bollettieri camp. But she hit the ball so consistently hard that soon all of the other women refused to take her on.

Monica, her brother, Zoltan, and their parents moved to the United States so Monica could attend tennis camp in Florida.

Bollettieri had another idea. He put his top male prospect—Jim Courier, a future number-one ranked men's player—up against Monica. Even though it was only a practice session, Monica again refused to ease up. After 15 minutes of dealing with the new girl's pounding shots, Courier too walked off the court. "I told Nick, never again. He could get another guinea pig," Courier said.

For the next year, Monica went through a strict solo training program under the watchful eyes of her two coaches, Nick Bollettieri and her father. They both felt that to limit the public pressure often faced by teenage stars, Monica should develop her game in practice rather than by playing in tournaments.

The family also wanted Monica to have as normal a life as possible. Rather than traveling around the world as a touring player, Monica attended local schools and earned straight A's.

Monica finally entered her first professional tournament—as an amateur—in the spring of 1987. She was 13 years old. Even though she lost in the second round, it was a good learning experience for her. Her coaches decided that she was almost ready for the "big time."

Monica turned professional the next year and won her first pro event, defeating Chris Evert, who had once been number one in the world. By the end of her first year on the professional tour, Monica jumped in the world rankings from number 88 to number nine. It was a remarkable rise. "In the beginning of the year, my realistic goal was to get into the top 50," she told reporters. "I didn't think I was going to reach the top 10!"

Early in 1990, Monica's ranking slipped a little, for a very unusual reason: she grew too fast. She had sprouted from 5-foot-4 to 5-foot-9 in less than a year. "Suddenly the net seemed a different height to me, and the racquet seemed lighter, like I was playing ping-pong," she explained. At around the same time, the Seleses decided to leave the Bollettieri camp and go out on their own, with Karolj continuing as Monica's coach and Zoltan becoming her business manager.

When Monica left the tennis camp in 1990, her brother, Zoltan, center, became her business manager and her father, Karolj, continued as her coach.

Monica quickly adapted to the physical and mental changes and began a string of 39 consecutive match victories. Along the way, she defeated Martina Navratilova, the world's number-two player, to win the Italian Open in May 1990. A few weeks later, she defeated number-one Steffi Graf to win the German Open. The victories helped Monica achieve number-three ranking in the world, behind Graf and Navratilova.

Monica's remarkable string ended in June with a defeat at Wimbledon, the famous tournament held in England. But she quickly bounced back at the United States Open in August, winning a dramatic five-set match against Gabriela Sabatini to become the youngest U.S. Open champ ever.

By then, only Steffi Graf stood between Monica and the number-one rank in the world. And when 17-year-old Monica won both the Australian and French Opens in early 1991, she became the youngest woman to move into the top spot.

Monica grew up fast. In just five years she went from being the Yugoslav champion to reaching the number one spot in the world, an achievement that makes her parents extremely proud.

The victories earned Monica money and fame. Suddenly her picture was on the cover of magazines around the world. She loved the attention, but not always the pressure that came with it.

That pressure really magnified when Monica mysteriously withdrew from Wimbledon in June 1991. In fact, she disappeared for two weeks, refusing to meet with tennis officials or the press to explain what was going on. Rumors spread that she was injured or pregnant or just ducking from Wimbledon, which she had never won, so she wouldn't lose her number-one ranking. Some reporters were particularly vicious toward the young star.

What had really happened was that Monica was confused. Her legs were hurting badly, and she had gotten conflicting diagnoses from several different doctors. One doctor advised an operation; another suggested a six-month rest; another said she should keep playing through the pain. After a six-week lay-off, she began practicing again, and in September captured her second consecutive U.S. Open title, tightening her hold on number one.

Monica Seles was back playing tennis and back to being a media star. The press and tennis world quickly warmed up to her again because of her style both on and off the court. That style includes willingly answering reporters' questions, cheerfully signing autographs, and making numerous public appearances in outfits that ranged from funky to elegant.

Throughout 1992 and into 1993, Monica kept a tight hold on her number-one ranking. Her greatest worry was that she might fall behind her top rival, Steffi Graf. Then a new fear took hold of Monica during a tennis tournament in Hamburg, Germany, in May 1993—fear for her life. During a

Monica Seles was carried from the court on a stretcher after she was stabbed in the back in 1993 in Hamburg, Germany.

break between games of a match, a German factory worker named Gunter Parche raced out of the stands and stabbed Monica in the back with a sharp knife, just missing her spinal cord. Parche said he attacked the tennis star to help Graf, his favorite player, become number one again.

The wound did more psychological than physical damage to Monica. She became very depressed and withdrew to her family home in Florida. Monica made an appearance during the U.S. Open in September, but only to wave to the fans. Later in the fall, she announced plans to return to competition at the Australian Open in January 1994, then decided she wasn't ready physically or mentally to come back. She remained away from the game for another year and a half.

During that time, Martina Navratilova, her childhood idol, visited her often to practice with her and to reassure her that she could still play top level tennis. Olympic track champion Jackie Joyner-Kersee and her husband and coach Bob Kersee helped her regain her physical fitness. And her father proved to be an inspiration when he triumphed in his own battle with stomach cancer.

"After seeing what he did, I told myself I had to try again," Monica said.

On August 15, 1995, Monica finally returned to tennis at the Canadian Open in Toronto. Even though she had been away for more than two years, she was ranked as the co-number-one player in the world, along with Steffi Graf. She quickly proved that she deserved the ranking by winning all five of her matches handily on the way to the Canadian championship.

Martina Navratilova, top photo, proved to be a strong supporter during Monica's two years away from tennis. Monica's father, center, was also an inspiration as he triumphed in his battle with cancer.

Following the title match, she told the Toronto fans, "For a long time everything was dark. Now I can see the sun."

Over the next six months, Monica reached the finals at the U.S. Open (losing a close match to Graf) and then won the Australian Open to earn her ninth Grand Slam title. Monica next took on the world, representing the United States in the 1996 Olympics in Atlanta. Monica breezed through the first three rounds against opponents from China, France, and Argentina before losing to Jana Novotna of Czechoslovakia in the quarter finals.

She rebounded within weeks when she reached the finals of the U.S. Open for the second straight year. She lost once again to Graf but played her rival virtually equal in skill and spirit.

Monica was back at last, though not quite the same as before. During her two years away, she had grown a little older, a little taller, and a little more cautious. But her energy and competitive spirit were back, and that was good news for the game of tennis, too.

"No matter how great a sport is, it needs superstars," said Navratilova. "When Monica was stabbed, we lost our number-one star. To have her back is a great boost."

Monica made a triumphant return to the tennis world with an abundance of energy and a competitive spirit.

VOICES

ON HER FAMILY AND CHILDHOOD:

"My father made tennis fun for me from the beginning. I was only seven or eight. Am I going to win a doll today? It was never about money. It was never if I beat anyone else."

Monica Seles

"It's nice to have my parents with me when I win or lose, too. I just couldn't imagine going to a tournament by myself, and my dad's my coach, so he'll always be there. I work with him the best, and I play the best when he's there."

Monica Seles

"I liked to do grown-up things even when I was 10 years old. I loved to dress up in my mom's high heels and put on lipstick. I put on all the black lace I could, and one hat after another. My mom would come home suddenly and she'd have a heart attack, pleading with me. 'Monica, please, wait until you are 17 or 18.'"

Monica Seles

"The word that comes to mind when I watch Monica Seles play is vicious. She seems to want to beat you 6-0, 6-0, while smiling all the way. Seles really has a killer instinct. She has the power game to match, too."

Arthur Ashe,
the late tennis champion

"Some TV viewers turn the sound off when she plays, as the effect (of her grunting) approaches Chinese water torture gone wild."

Cindy Hahn, tennis writer

"She is every bit a champion, and she never quits. She does not look like she has the legs to cover the court the way she does. Seles will come up on a ball in the middle of the court, come up on it after a long run, and will not seem to have any kind of play, except perhaps to push the ball back somewhere. And here it is she guns her best shot right past you. I think of all the other baseliners I have seen, not one of them could have stayed in there with Seles."

Mike Lupica, sportswriter

Monica is enjoying the game of tennis again. She has a slashing, two-handed forehand and she never slows down on the court.

"Graf is the best athlete on the tour, but mentally Seles is by far the strongest. She's a ferocious competitor, and her concentration is so keen on every point. She doesn't look like she's going to let any shot go. There are certainly ways to beat Seles, but you've got to play awfully well."

Tom Gullikson,
former tennis coach

ON THE ATTACK IN GERMANY:

"We've had threats to Monica before, and to other players as well. But this is bizarre. You can't imagine someone who would take sport to such an absurd level. Someone has broken through an invisible barrier (between athletes and fans). It's not just a threat. Something actually happened that changes everything. Things are not the same today as they were yesterday."

Gerard Smith, executive director, Women's Tennis Association

"This is something we all live with. It's the price we have to pay [for our fame]."

Steffi Graf, tennis rival

When she returned to tennis competition after a two-year absence, Monica reached the number-one spot again, sharing the honor with Steffi Graf, bottom photo.

"You know, for two and a half years I practiced and it didn't matter if I made a shot or I didn't. Now, when it's 30-30 in a match, it matters. You've got to make it."

Monica Seles

"I decided I was going to play tennis, calm down and have fun. I've always been strong mentally, able to block out everything but the racquet and the ball. It's going to take a while. If it doesn't take a while, that's great."

Monica Seles

Monica worked hard to stay on top of her game. She won her ninth Grand Slam title at the Australian Open, and she proudly represented the United States at the 1996 Summer Olympics.

"Glamour has finally returned to
the game."

Ted Tinling, tennis historian

"When I wake up in the morning,
I'm not always sure who I'm going
to be that day. I want to live as
normal a life as I can have. I'm
determined not to miss out on
being young."

Monica Seles

"Monica is a trend-setter. She has
such self-assurance and poise for
someone her age. And it's no fake
creation. That's genuinely her."

*Chris Evert,
former women's tennis champion*

"Everything is too simple in tennis
now. Wouldn't it be neat to be a
mystery woman and bring high
fashion back to the sport? To be
like Suzanne Lenglen, like
Madonna, out there but untouch-
able, unreachable?"

Monica Seles

ON HER AMBITION OF BECOMING AN ACTRESS:

"I love the idea of getting into somebody else's life, pretending I'm somebody else. Maybe I'll be another Grace Kelly, or Marlene Dietrich—a Julia Roberts or a Michelle Pfeiffer."

Monica Seles

Monica Seles has self-assurance and poise. She dreams of being a mystery women and a movie star.

OVATIONS